CHINESE LIGHT MEALS & SNACKS

CHINESE LIGHT MEALS & SNACKS

Sumi Hatano

SHUFUNOTOMO/JAPAN PUBLICATIONS

First printing, 1992

© Copyright 1992 in Japan
by Sumi Hatano
Photographs by Takehiko Takei
Book design by Momoyo Nishimura

Published by Shufunotomo Co., Ltd.,
2-9, Kanda Surugadai, Chiyoda-ku,
Tokyo, 101 Japan

DISTRIBUTORS:
United States: Kodansha America, Inc.,
through Farrar, Straus & Giroux,
19 Union Square West, New York, NY 10003.
Canada: Fitzenry & Whiteside Ltd.,
91 Granton Drive, Richmond Hill,
Ontario L4B 2N5.
British Isles & European Continent: Premier Book
Marketing Ltd.,
1 Gower Street, London WC1E 6HA.
Australia and New Zealand: Bookwise International,
54 Crittenden Road, Findon, South Australia 5023.
The Far East and Japan: Japan Publications Trading Co., Ltd.,
1-2-1, Sarugaku-cho, Chiyoda-ku, Tokyo 101.

Printed in Japan
ISBN 0-87040-888-7

PREFACE

We have already published several cookbooks for Chinese dishes which are delicious and easy to prepare at home. A series of our cookery books has been popular abroad as well as in Japan.

Since the late 1980s, Japanese have become increasingly interested in healthy as well as tasty cooking.

For this reason, we have decided to focus on a low-calorie dish, Chinese rice porridge (congee in Chinese) which keeps you warm in winter and is kind to your stomach in summer.

Included in this book about Chinese rice porridge are a variety of side dishes, such as dim sum and pickles.

This volume includes various kinds of rice porridge, ranging from Guangdong rice porridge with abundant shellfish and Chaozhou rice porridge, which is relatively hard and less sticky, to thick Shanghai rice porridge.

Chinese rice porridge has been widely loved since ancient times in China. We hope that you will enjoy adding Chinese rice porridge to your busy lifestyle, to make your meals more stimulating.

To make Guangdong-styled porridge you stir the ingredients until they form a paste. It may contain fish dumplings, chicken livers or deep-fried breadsticks to make it more nutritions. People eat this not only for breakfast but also as a light snack in the afternoon or for a casual evening snack.

Shanghai porridge is made by boiling rice gently without changing its original shape.

In the north and southwest regions of China, there is "light porridge," which is made by adding water to leftover rice and boiling.

In Beijing, you can often see people eating a delicious *man-tou* (Chinese-style bun) with a light rice porridge instead of milk. Old and sick people eat medicinal porridges, and many others eat those same porridges for prevention of illness. In the long history of China, the custom of eating porridge has been prevalent and, because of the country's huge land area, each region has developed different varieties of this popular dish.

When you make a trip to China, you will be served porridge for breakfast in many hotels. To add to your enjoyment, you may have many side dishes such as sliced ham and sausage, fried egg and vegetables, and fried or boiled peanuts with warm steaming porridge.

There is a saying in China, "Purify the intestines and clean the stomach." At the start of the day, people eat porridge for this purpose.

Such porridges probably play a big role in nursing, resting and protecting the stomach when many oily Chinese dishes have been eaten. Whether one is rich or poor, whether king or beggar, in China all people love to eat rice porridge. It is low in calories, easy to digest, warming in winter, by increasing perspiration helpful in preventing heat prostration in summer, and has all the good qualities needed to combat the stress that accumulates in daily life.

Sumi Hatano

CONTENTS

● All recipes are for four servings.

SEASONINGS AND SPICES

"Hua-jiao"
(Szechuan peppercorns) 花椒
Dried brown Szechuan peppercorns. Whole peppers are used for boiling meat. Toasted and ground powder peppers are also available. Powdered and salted peppers (*hua-jiao-yan*) are served with deep fried dishes. They are available in bottles for table use.　　(1)

"Tian-mian-jinag"
(Sweet brown bean paste) 甜麵醬
Black sweet bean paste made from flour. This thick paste is served with Beijing duck and grilled pork. Also used for stir-fried meat, as well as vegetables and noodles. Heated Japanese red bean paste diluted with soup stock and sugar can be substituted.　　(2)

"Ba-jiao"
(Star anise) 八角
Dried fruit of the Chinese anise. Star-shaped. Used as a spice for boiling pork, liver and kidneys, etc.　　(3)

"Dou-chi"
(Fermented soy beans) 豆豉
Black dried fermented beans. Made of steamed beans fermented in flour, salt and malt. Chopped beans are used as a seasoning for stir-fried dishes or boiled dishes. Since the taste is quite salty, be careful about adding additional salt to dishes with this ingredient. Japanese fermented beans such as daitokuji beans can be substituted. *Dou-chi* produced in Szechuan is used in *Ma-po-dou-fu*.　　(4)

(1)

(2)

(3)

(4)

(5)

(6)

(7)

(8)

"Hao-you"
(Oyster sauce) 蠔油

Supernatant fluid taken from raw oysters fermented by salt. It is frequently used in Cantonese cooking, where it is prized for its exquisite flavor. It is sold in bottles mainly from China and Hong Kong, although some is produced in Japan. (5)

"La-you"
(Chili pepper oil) 辣油

Hot seasoning made from vegetable oil, such as sesame oil, to which peppers have been added. It is mainly used at the table. It is sold in bottles, or can be made easily at home. Use 2 or 3 whole red peppers unseeded and 5 tablespoons oil. Chop peppers finely. Heat oil in a frying pan and fry the chopped peppers slowly until the oil absorbs the flavor of the peppers. Strain the oil through gauze. (6)

"Zhi-ma-jiang"
(Sesame seed paste) 芝麻醬

A sticky paste made from white sesames. It has a rich, aromatic flavor, and is used as a sauce for boiled pork, steamed chicken and many other items. Available in bottles. As oil often rises to the top, shake it well before using. (7)

"Dou-ban-jiang"
(Brown bean paste) 豆板醬

This is made from broad beans fermented in flour, salt and malt. There are several kinds of chili paste. Chili bean paste used in Szechuan cooking has red peppers added to it. This latter type of paste is sold in Japan. (8)

RICE PORRIDGES

In China, rice porridge is very popular and there are many rice porridge restaurants. Softly boiled plain rice together with 4–6 side dishes is a tasty and healthy way to start a new day. Apart from this, rice porridge is sometimes served after dinner as the very last dish, a habit similar to the Japanese custom of serving a broth made of boiled rice with tea.

There are various kinds of rice porridge in China. The basic rice porridge, however, is a plain white one, which can be made either by boiling uncooked rice or by reboiling left-over rice. This book concentrates on the former.

Once you learn how to successfully cook a basic plain rice porridge, you can experiment with other kinds, such as rice porridge mixed with fish, meat, herbs and many other healthy ingredients.

Plain Porridge,
p. 10
Fried Eggs in "Fu-ru",
P. 58
Giant White Radish
in Soy Sauce,
P. 55
Fried Peanuts,
P. 10
Chinese Parsley
Zha-cai (Sichuan
preserved Vegetables),
sliced
Pi-dan, cut in wedges

Basic Porridges
Plain Porridge

The trick to making authentic rice porridge, which is made from scratch by boiling rice grains, is to wash rice grains well, but quickly, and boil them in a heavy pan over low heat. The amount of water to cook rice should be adjusted to your taste—a little more, if you like it soft. Nothing is to be added to plain rice porridge, even salt.

Ingredients:
1 cup rice
10–12 cups water

Method:
1. Put rice in earthen pot or other heavy pan. Pour in plenty of water, and stir quickly two or three times. Drain. (1–3)
2. Stir rice again, firmly, with fingers. (4)
3. Pour in plenty of water again, and drain quickly. Stir again. Repeat this until the water becomes clean. (5)
4. When water is clean, drain well and pour in 10–12 cups of water. Put the pan over high heat without a lid. (6)
5. When it comes to a boil, reduce heat. Cook slowly for 45 to 60 minutes without stirring. Cover and steam for about 10 minutes.

Notes: When washing rice, do it quickly. The first water, especially, should be thrown away immediately after stirring, so the rice does not taste like bran. Keep the heat on high until the water comes to a boil, but lower it afterwards. If you stir during cooking, the porridge becomes gluey.

Fried Peanuts

Fried peanuts go well with plain rice porridge. Place peanuts with shells in hot frying oil, and deep-fry until light brown. Be careful not to burn.

White Meat Fish Porridge

Seasoned fresh fish is steamed in porridge. This is a Guangdong-style dish.

Ingredients:
1 cup rice
10–12 cups water
200 g (7 oz.) white fish fillet, thinly sliced (porgy, etc.)
Seasonings:
   1/3 stalk of green onion
   3 cm (1/2 inch) ginger root
   1 tablespoon Chinese rice wine or saké
   1 tablespoon soy sauce
Salt and pepper
Chinese parsley for garnish

Method:
1. Wash and rinse rice. Add 10–12 cups of water. Bring to a boil over high heat and then simmer for about 1 hour over low heat.
2. In the meantime, prepare fish mixture. (1)
3. Chop green onion and ginger into fine pieces.
4. Arrange fish slices in skillet or bowl, and sprinkle with green onion and ginger mixture.
Sprinkle with sake and soy sauce to season. (2)
5. When rice becomes porridge-like, season with salt and pepper. Add fish mixture along with green onions and ginger. Turn off heat, cover, and steam for about 5 minutes. (3–4)
6. Arrange in dish, and garnish with Chinese parsley.

Oyster Porridge

Select full and firm fresh oysters. Fried peanuts add unexpected flavor.

Ingredients:
300 g (2/3 lb.) oysters, taken out of shells
1/4 cup dried shrimp
1 cup rice
10–12 cups water
1/2 cup peanuts with skin
Salt and pepper
Oil for deep-frying

Method:
1. Wash dried shrimp quickly and soak them in 1 cup of water.
2. Wash oysters in lightly salted water, to get rid of shell bits and dirt. Then wash them quickly in running water. Cut big ones into two.   (1–2)
3. Put the oysters in boiling water and then drain quickly.   (3)
4. Wash rice and add 10–11 cups of water. Add shrimp with the water they were soaked in. Place over high heat.   (4)
5. When it comes to a boil, reduce heat, and simmer for about 1 hour. When the rice gets gruel-like, add oysters. Stir once, and season with salt and pepper.   (5)
6. Deep-fry peanuts in hot oil quickly until they skins turn light brown, and sprinkle over porridge in bowls.   (6)

Seafood Porridge

This is a deluxe rice porridge with plenty of seafood. Light-tasting seafood porridge is not heavy on the stomach and is very nutritious.

Ingredients:

1 cup rice
12 cups water
200 g (7 oz.) whitemeat fish

A {
Dash of salt
1 tablespoon Chinese rice wine or saké
1 teaspoon cornstarch
}

4 prawns
4 scallops

B {
1 teaspoon squeezed ginger juice
1 tablespoon Chinese rice wine or saké
}

1 squid
Oil for deep-frying
Salt and pepper
Some kaiware (daikon sprouts)

Method:

1. Remove the skin and bones of whitemeat fish, and grind the meat in a ceramic mortar. Mix with A, and form into 2.5 cm (1 inch) dumplings. (1–2)

2. Remove the skin of prawns, leaving the tails. Remove also the black veins in the back. Wash the prawns quickly, drain well using paper towels, and deep-fry them in medium temperature oil.

3. Remove the whitish skin of scallops and cut them in half horizontally. Sprinkle with B mixture, and set aside for a while so scallops will absorb the flavor. Wipe off moisture and deep-fry them quickly. (3–4)

4. Remove squid's guts and legs. Cut into one flat piece, and remove its thin skin. Wipe the squid with a cloth Make incisions to 2/3 of thickness of squid in a diagonal pattern. Then cut into bite-size pieces. Dry and deep-fry in oil over medium heat. (5–6)

5. Wash rice, and add 12 cups of water. Place over high heat. When it comes to a boil, add dumplings. Reduce heat, and

cook on low heat so it doesn't boil. Remove scum as it rises to surface.

6. Cook for about 50 minutes. Then season with salt and pepper, and add prawns, scallops and squid. Serve in dishes, and garnish with daikon sprouts.

Rice Porridge with Pork Dumplings

The tasty pork dumplings enrich the flavor of the rice porridge. Pound the ground pork firmly before using, so that the dumplings are smooth on the palate.

Ingredients:

1 cup rice
10–12 cups water
Meat dumplings:
   300 g (2/3 lb.) ground pork
   2 tablespoons dried shrimp
   1 tablespoon Chinese rice wine
     or saké
   2 tablespoons soy sauce
   1 tablespoon cornstarch
   1/2 cup water
1 bunch of greens (chrysanthemum
   leaves, etc.)
Salt and pepper

Method:

1. Wash rice well and drain in colander.

2. Wash dried shrimp quickly, and soak in 1/2 cup of water. Cut them into small pieces. (1–2)

3. Chop ground pork with a knife, and then pound with back of knife to smooth it out. (3)

4. Add dried shrimp to the ground pork. Add the rice wine and soy sauce. Mix well. Add cornstarch and pour in 1/2 cup water to soften. (4)

5. Put rice in earthen pot or other heavy pan and pour in 10–12 cups of water. Place over high heat.

6. When water comes to a boil, grip ground pork mixture in the hand, and squeeze between thumb and index finger to make dumplings of 2.5 cm (1 inch) in diameter. Drop them into the boiling water. (5–6)

7. Parboil the greens with salt and drain.

8. Reduce heat to low and simmer for 45 minutes to one hour. When rice becomes porridge-like, season with salt and pepper. Add the greens.

Rice Porridge with Chicken

The chicken is boiled first, and then cooked in porridge slowly for a long time, so the meat becomes tender enough to easily fall from the bones.

Ingredients:
1 cup rice
12 cups water
350 g (3/4 lb.) chicken with bones
300 g (2/3 lb.) Chinese cabbage
1-1/2 teaspoon salt
Dash of pepper

Method:
1. Cut up chicken into easy-to-eat pieces. Boil them in plenty of hot water. When the meat turns whitish, drain in colander. (1)
2. Parboil Chinese cabbage in boiling water and drain. Cut into 5 cm (2 inch) lengths.
3. Wash rice and add 12 cups of water. Put over high heat. When it comes to a boil, add chicken and Chinese cabbage. (2)
4. When it comes to a boil again, reduce heat and simmer for about 1 hour. Remove scum as it rises to the surface. Season with salt and pepper. (3)

Porridge with Dried Scallops

This is a delicious porridge, made with dried scallops which have been soaked in water overnight. The water used to reconstitute the scallops makes good soup, so this is also used and replaces some portion of the water necessary to make the porridge.

Ingredients:
1 cup rice
9–11 cups water
5–6 dried scallops
1 tablespoon Chinese rice wine
    or saké
1 tablespoon minced watercress or
    parsley
1-1/2 teaspoon salt
Dash of pepper

Method:
1. Soak dried scallops in about 1 cup of water just to cover, and leave overnight. (1)
2. Wash rice and add 9–11 cups of water, and place over high heat. When it comes to a boil, add the scallops along with the water used to soak them. (2)
3. Simmer for about 1 hour after scallops are added. When it becomes porridge-like, season with salt and pepper, and sprinkle with minced watercress or parsley.

Rice Porridge with Pickled Vegetables

This porridge is made with pickled vegetables and flavored with dried shrimp. Do not use vegetables with a high salt content.

Ingredients:
1 cup rice
11 cups water
200 g (7 oz.) pickled vegetables
1/3 cup dried shrimp
1 to 1-1/2 teaspoons salt

Method:
1. Wash pickled vegetables quickly in running water. Drain well and mince into fine pieces.   (1–2)
2. Wash dried shrimp quickly. Add water just to cover and soak for 20 minutes.
3. Wash rice and add 11 cups of water. Cook over high heat unti it comes to a boil, then reduce heat to low.
4. Simmer for about 30 minutes. Add shrimp along with water used to soak it, and simmer for another 20 to 30 minutes.
5. Add pickled vegetables, just before the gruel is done, and stir quickly once. Check the taste, and if necessary, season with salt.

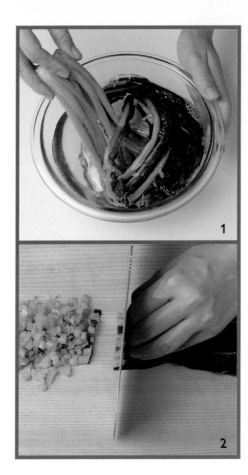

Medicinal Porridges

Porridge with Taro Yam and Lotus Seeds

This porridge, seasoned with sugar, is thought to have a calming effect and to elevate one's mood. It is also said to be effective for loss of appetite, fatigue, sleeplessness, and anemia.

Ingredients:
1 cup rice
10–12 cups water
200 g (7 oz.) taro yam
1/2 cup lotus seeds
1/2 cup raisins
100 g (3-1/2 oz.) sugar
Dash of salt

Method:
1. Peel taro yams, slice into thin bite-sized pieces, and boil them until soft.
(1)
2. Boil lotus seeds until soft.
3. Wash raisins quickly and drain in a colander. (2)
4. Wash rice well, add 10–12 cups of water and place it over high heat. When it comes to a boil, reduce heat and simmer for about 1 hour.
5. Add taro yams, raisins, and lotus seeds to porridge and stir quickly. Season with sugar and salt.

Note: Lotus seeds are soft when they are young. But older ones which have been dried are used more often. Boil them before adding to porridge, soups, or stews. (A)

1

2

A

Chestnut Porridge

In China, people often make sweet porridges with chestnuts, ginkgo nuts, pinenuts and dried persimmons. Chestnuts are a medicine for the kidney. They are said to be effective for dullness in the legs and hips, back-aches and hip-aches, ringing ears, and loss of hair.

Ingredients:

1 cup rice
10–12 cups water
200 g (7 oz.) shelled chestnuts
200 g (7 oz.) shelled ginkgo nuts
Syrup:
   1 cup sugar
   1 cup water
   100 g (3-1/2 oz.) green plums
    (see Note)
1-1/4 cups sugar
Dash of salt

Method:

1. Remove shells and skins of chestnuts. Cut big ones in half, and use small ones whole.
2. Remove shells of ginkgo nuts. Boil them and remove skins by scraping them with a spoon.
3. Bring syrup made of sugar and water to a boil. Add green plums and cook until they become soft. (1–2)
4. Wash rice and add 10–12 cups of water. Cook over high heat until it comes to a boil. Then reduce heat, and cook for 1 hour.
5. When it becomes porridge-like, add chestnuts, ginkgo-nuts, and plums, and cook for about 5 minutes. Then add sugar and salt. (3)

Note: Green plums are used to make plum wine. These plums are effective in recovering from fatigue, promoting appetite, reducing fever, healing pains, and preventing colds. Make plum wine in June when green plums are on the market. Green plums can be replaced by regular plums.

Milk Porridge

This is a smooth, sweet porridge made with milk. Milk contains many good quality proteins. Each component can be digested to a high degree, and they help organs function smoothly. Milk is also a very good source of calcium and strengthens bones.

Ingredients:
1 cup rice
10–11 cups water
1 cup milk
3–4 tablespoons sugar

Method:
1. Wash rice and add 10–11 cups water. Bring to a boil over high heat, then reduce heat and simmer for about 40 minutes without covering.　　(1)
2. When it begins to be porridge-like, add milk and stir lightly. Boil over low heat for about 10 more minutes, and season with sugar to taste.　　(2)

Chinese Red Bean Porridge

The outer skin of red beans 赤小豆 (*chi-xiao-dou*) promotes urination and relieves constipation. It also prevents swelling, beriberi, dryness of mouth, and nutritional disorders. In Japan, there was a custom in olden times to eat red bean gruel on the 1st and 15th of every month to aid nutrition.

Ingredients:
1 cup rice
10–12 cups water
1/2 cup Chinese red beans
  (*chi-xiao-dou*)
1-1/2 teaspoons salt

Method:
1. Wash red beans and discard worm-eaten ones, dirt, and sand. Add water just to cover, and place pot over high heat.

2. When it comes to a boil, add about 1 cup of water. When it comes to a boil again, reduce heat to medium. Remove bubbles and scum upon the surface.

3. Add water 3–4 times to keep beans always covered in water. Simmer for 40 minutes to 1 hour, until the beans soften. Drain.

4. Wash rice, and add 10–12 cups of water. Place pot over high heat until it comes to a boil, then simmer over low heat until it becomes porridge-like. Add beans and stir. Season with salt.

Chinese Date Porridge

Chinese dried dates 紅棗 (*hong-zao*) promote the functions of the intestines, as well as of the stomach. They are effective as a tonic and nutritious food for weak stomachs, poor circulation, and menstrual disorders.

Ingredients:
1 cup rice
10–12 cups water
15 Chinese dried dates (50 g; 2 oz.)
2–4 tablespoons sugar
Dash of salt

Method:
1. Wash Chinese dried dates to clean. Add plenty of water and simmer over low heat until they become soft.
2. Wash rice and add 10–12 cups of water. Place pot over high heat. When it comes to a boil, reduce heat to low. Simmer for about 1 hour.
3. Add Chinese dates when the rice is porridge-like, and cook for about 2 or 3 minutes. Season with sugar and salt.

Note: Chinese dried dates have been used as a medicine in China since olden times. Dried dates are sometimes made into jam to fill buns. They can be steamed or preserved in sugar.

Coix Seed Porridge

This is a porridge made with coix or edible jobs tears seeds, 薏苡仁 (*i-i-jen*), which are more effective for circulation than rice. Coix seeds promote the physiological functions of the body, so they are not only nutritious, but also effective in preventing coughs and phlegm, and in curing weak or swollen limbs.

Ingredients:
1 cup coix seeds

8 cups water
50 g (2 oz.) almonds
Dash of salt

Method:
1. Wash coix seeds, and add 8 cups of water. Place pot over high heat. When it comes to a boil, reduce heat, and simmer for about 40 minutes.
2. When using whole-style almonds with skins, soak them in hot water, and remove the skins.
3. When coix seeds become soft, season with salt, and add almonds.

Note: Coix or Adlay (Latin: *Coix lachryma-Jobi*) 薏苡 (*i-i*) belong to the gramineae family, and their grains are an oblong-shape. The dried grains, with husks removed, are called 薏苡仁 (*i-i-jen*). Those in husks which haven't been threshed are first roasted, then simmered to make tea. For cooking purposes, use threshed coix seeds.

Glutinous Rice and Corn Porridge

This is a porridge made with glutinous rice, and it tastes a little different from porridge made with regular, non-glutinous rice. This is very popular in Southeast Asia, and is served as a dessert. Corn is effective in promoting lung functions, mental stability, and the smooth functioning of the intestines and stomach. So it is good for high cholesterol, and for heart and vascular diseases. It's also said to be effective in preventing cancer.

Ingredients:
1 cup glutinous rice
8 cups water
1 medium-sized can; 150 g (1/3 lb.),
    whole corn
2 cups sugar

Method:
1. Wash rice and add 8 cups of water. Cook over high heat at first, and reduce heat when it comes to a boil. Simmer for about 1 hour.
2. When it becomes porridge-like, add drained corn. Add sugar to taste.

LIGHT DISHES

Since rice porridge is rather light on the stomach, it is recommended that you add several other side dishes for nourishment.

Serve vegetables as well as meat and fish. A slightly salty dish may go well with rice porridge.

On the following pages are some dishes which go wonderfully with rice porridge.

Vegetable Dishes

Stir-Fried Bean Sprouts and Leeks

Simple fried vegetables are indispensable for serving with pooridge, to aid nutrition and add flavor. Bean sprouts should not be over-fried or they will not remain crisp.

Ingredients:
400 g (15 oz.) bean sprouts
50 g (2 oz.) yellow scallion
　韮黄 (*jiu-huang*)
2 tablespoons salad oil
1 teaspoon salt
1/4 teaspoon sugar

Method:
1. Remove the bean sprouts' black heads and stringy tails. Wash well and drain in colander. (1)
2. Wash and drain yellow scallion. Cut them into 5 cm (2-inch) lengths.
3. Fill wok 70% full of oil and place over high heat. When the oil gets hot, put in bean sprouts and stir-fry. Add leeks and fry more. (2)
4. Add salt and sugar, and fry quickly. Cover with a lid and steam for 1 or 2 minutes. When the sprouts become clear in color, remove from fire. (3)

Note: Removing heads and tails of bean sprouts will make prettier fries. A dash of sugar makes for a smoother taste.

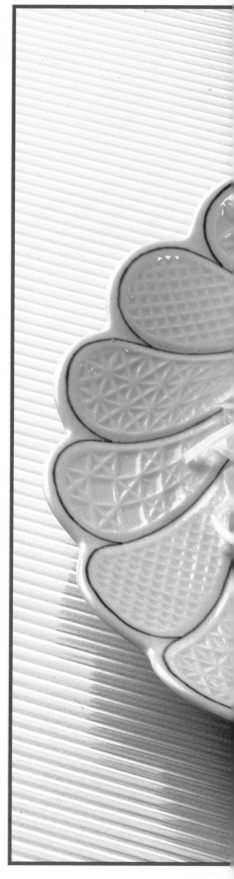

Sautéed Pea Sprouts

These pea sprouts 豆苗 (*dou-miao*) are specially grown in China for use in cooking. If they are unavailable, other leafy green vegetables can be used, such as celery cabbage 青梗菜 (*qing-geng-cai*) or spinach.

Ingredients:

200 g (7 oz.) pea sprouts
2 tablespoons salad oil
   1 teaspoon salt
   1 cup water

Method:

1. If pea sprouts have long tendrils, remove them. Wash well and drain. (1)

2. Heat 2 tablespoons salad oil in wok. Put in pea sprouts and sauté quickly over high heat. (2)

3. Add salt, and pour in water. Cover with lid and steam for 1–2 minutes. (3–5)

4. When soft, pour off liquid and transfer to serving plate.

Note: These sprouts are tender, and people enjoy their flavor, which resembles garden peas, and also their beautiful green color. They are a delicacy, often used in special menus for parties. Use only the upper 10 cm (4 in.) or so of the shoots.

Stir-Fried Eggplants and Tomatoes

This dish can be made quickly, using ingredients that combine well.

Ingredients:
4 eggplants
1 ripe tomato
4 eggs
1 teaspoon minced garlic
Seasoning mixture:
1/2 teaspoon salt
2 teaspoons sugar
1 tablespoon soy sauce
1 tablespoon Chinese rice wine or saké
1 teaspoon tabasco
2 teaspoons cornstarch
4 tablespoons salad oil
Oil for deep-frying

Method:

1. Wash eggplants, remove stems, and cut them into half lengthwise, then dice into bite-sized pieces. Fill pan 70% full with oil and heat to medium. Deep-fry.

2. Wash tomatoes, remove the stems, and dice into bite-sized pieces.

3. Beat eggs well.

4. Heat 2 tablespoons oil in a wok over high heat, pour in eggs and stir-fry until eggs begin to thicken. Remove eggs from the pan, and set them aside.

5. Heat 2 tablespoons of oil in a wok over high heat, and sauté minced garlic. When it begins to smell savory, add tomatoes, then eggplants, and stir-fry.

6. Add the seasoning mixture, and stir-fry quickly. Add eggs, and mix them quickly.

Sautéed String Beans in Chicken Fat

String beans are fried first with salt and water in Chinese style, then cooked with chicken fat and soup, to deepen and enrich the flavor.

Ingredients:

300 g (2/3 lb.) string beans
  1 teaspoon salt
  1 cup water
  2 tablespoons salad oil
30 g (1 oz.) chicken fat
Soup:
  1 cup chicken broth
  1 teaspoon salt
  1 teaspoon sugar

Method:

1. String the beans and cut into two or three pieces.

2. Heat 2 tablespoons salad oil in a wok over high heat. Sauté string beans quickly. Add salt and water. Cover and cook for 2–3 minutes. Set string beans aside on plate.

3. Drain the wok. Put it over heat again, and melt chicken fat. Add sautéed string beans, and stir-fry again quickly. Add soup and cover. Cook over medium-high heat until string beans are soft.

Stir-Fried Asparagus and Ham

This is a delicate vegetable dish, seasoned lightly with soup and thickened with cornstarch. The fine combination of light-tasting asparagus and ham can be enjoyed from spring through summer.

Ingredients:

2 bunches; 400 g (1 lb.) green asparagus
   1 teaspoon salt
   1 cup water
150 g (1/3 lb.) ham
3 tablespoons salad oil
1/3 cup chicken broth
Seasoning mixture:
   1 tablespoon Chinese rice wine or saké
   1 teaspoon sugar
   1/2 teaspoon salt
   Dash of pepper
   2–3 drops sesame oil
2 teaspoons cornstarch dissolved in 4 teaspoons water

Method:

1. Cut off hard ends of asparagus and peel lower 1/3. Slice into 5 cm (2-inch) lengths. (1)

2. Slice ham thinly.

3. Heat 2 tablespoons of salad oil in wok and sauté asparagus. Add salt and water, cover and cook until tender. Remove from wok.

4. Clean the wok. Heat 1 tablespoon of salad oil in wok. Stir-fry asparagus and ham quickly. Add seasoning mixture and broth. (2)

5. Cover with lid, and cook for a while. Thicken with dissolved cornstarch. (3)

Deep-Fried Eggplants with Sauce

Fried eggplants are served with a savory hot sauce. Eggplants are scored to make them easier to cook, nicer on the tongue, and better to look at.

Ingredients:
6 eggplants
Oil for deep-drying
Sauce:
  1 red chili pepper
  1 clove garlic
  1 tablespoon white sesame seeds
  1 tablespoon vinegar
  1 tablespoon sugar
  2 tablespoons soy sauce
  1 tablespoon sesame oil

Method:
1. Remove seeds from red chili pepper, and mince into tiny pieces. Mince the garlic. Toast the sesame seeds.
2. Mix liquid ingredients well, add chili pepper, garlic and sesame seeds and mix further.
3. Cut stems off eggplants, and cut them in half lengthwise. (1)
4. Place the cut sides on cutting board, and slice horizontally about halfway through, at 3 mm (1/10-inch) intervals. Cut into 2.5 cm-(1-inch)-wide pieces. (2)
5. Fill pan 70% full of oil and heat to medium. Add eggplants. When the scored sections open, remove from pan and drain oil. (3–4)
6. Arrange on plate, and cover with sauce prepared in advance. Serve hot.

Note: Cut eggplants just before you deep-fry them. Wipe them with cloth if they get wet before frying.

Mixed Celery and Carrots

Savory sesame oil adds to the taste. If left for 10 to 15 minutes before serving, the taste becomes richer.

Ingredients:
400 g (15 oz.) celery
1 carrot
Seasonings:
   1 teaspoon sugar
   1/2 teaspoon salt
   1 teaspoon sesame oil

Method:
1. Remove strings from celery, and slice into 7–8 mm (1/3 inch) thick pieces.
2. Slice carrot into 5 mm (1/5 inch) thick pieces. If you wish, give the carrot pieces a pretty shape, such as a flower blossom, either by cutting each individual piece into shape after it's sliced, or by scoring the carrot vertically 5 times before you slice it.
3. Mix the seasonings in a bowl. Marinate the celery and carrots. Let stand for 15 minutes before serving.

Tossed Watercress and Mushrooms with Chinese Matrimony-vine berries

A little tart-tasting watercress salad is well suited to accompany special porridges containing meat or fish. This dish contains Chinese matrimony-vine berries, which are good for the health.

Ingredients:
2 bunches of watercress
2 bags of golden needle mushrooms
2 tablespoons dried Chinese matrimony-vine berries
Vinegar mixture:
  3 tablespoons vinegar
  1 teaspoon salt
  2 teaspoons sugar
  1/2 teaspoon sesame oil

Method:
1. Wash Chinese matrimony-vine berries and soak in lukewarm water to soften.
2. Wash watercress, dry, and cut into 4 cm (1 1/2 inch) lengths.
3. Cut off hard ends of golden needle mushrooms and separate them.
4. Place vinegar mixture in a bowl, add watercress, golden needle mushrooms, and Chinese matrimony-vine berries and mix well. Let stand for a while to blend the flavors.

Note: Dried Chinese matrimony-vine berries (*Lycium chinense* Miller; Lycii fructus) are sold at Chinese food stores and pharmacies. Their Chinese name is 枸杞子 (*gou-qi-zi*). They are said to be good for recovering from fatigue, for strength and nutrition, and for the eyes.

Sweet and Sour Turnips

This is a dish tinted with hot red chili pepper. It is easily made, by only cutting and mixing. It's ready to eat in just 20–30 minutes.

Ingredients:

5–6 turnips
2 teaspoons salt
1 medium carrot
1 red chili pepper
Vinegar mixture:
1/2 cup vinegar
1/2 cup sugar
1/2 teaspoon sesame oil

Method:

1. Peel turnips, and slice thinly. Big ones should be cut in half and then sliced thinly.

2. Place turnips in a bowl, and sprinkle with salt. Let stand for a while. When they become softened, wash, and drain well in a colander.

3. Cut carrot into julienne strips. Remove seeds from red chili pepper, and mince it into tiny pieces.

4. Put vinegar mixture in a bowl and add turnips and carrot. Toss occasionally, and let sit for 15 minutes.

Pounded Cucumber with Soy Sauce

This is a very simple dish in which cucumbers are pounded and seasoned with soy sauce. Served cold, this is a refreshing dish with a touch of ginger.

Ingredients:
4 cucumbers
4–5 thin slices ginger
1 red chili pepper
1/2 cup soy sauce
1 teaspoon sesame oil

Method:
1. Cut cucumbers lengthwise into halves, and then into three pieces crosswise. Pound cucumbers with the back of a heavy knife to bring out the flavor.
2. Cut ginger thinly lengthwise. Remove seeds from red chili pepper and mince it.
3. Place pounded cucumber on plate. Sprinkle with ginger and red chili pepper mixture and add soy sauce and sesame oil.

Marinated Celery and Scallops

Canned scallops are used to enrich the taste of the dish. The amount of brown bean paste 豆板醬 (*dou-ban-jiang*) should be adjusted to taste.

Ingredients:
300 g (2/3 lb.) celery
1 bunch watercress
1 small can scallops

Vinegar mixture:
   3 tablespoons vinegar
   2 tablespoons sugar
   1 tablespoon soy sauce
   1/4 teaspoon salt
   1 teaspoon brown bean paste
      (*dou-ban-jiang*)
   1 teaspoon sesame oil

Method:
1. Remove strings from celery, and cut lengthwise into 5 cm-(2 inch-) long pieces and slice thinly.
2. Wash watercress well, drain, and cut into 4 cm-(1-1/2 inch-) long pieces.
3. Put vinegar mixture ingredients in bowl, and mix well. Add scallops after flaking, then add celery and watercress and mix well.

54

Giant White Radish in Soy Sauce

Crisp pickles are an indispensable dish to accompany porridge. If possible, use giant white radishes or daikon that have been dried for a day or two.

Ingredients:
1/2 stalk, 600 g (1 1/3 lb.) giant white radish or daikon
2 tablespoons sugar
1/2 cup soy sauce
1/2 teaspoon sesame oil

Method:
1. Cut the giant white radish into 1 cm (1/2 inch) rectangular shapes, and dry it in a colander for a day and a night in a cool, dry place.
2. Put radish pieces in a bowl. Sprinkle with sugar, and pour on soy sauce just to cover.
3. Turn over occasionally, and soak from 30 minutes to 3 hours. (See note). When radish has absorbed the flavor, put onto plate and sprinkle with sesame.

Note: Giant white radish can absorb flavors in about 30 minutes, but it's better to leave for 2–3 hours.

Egg Dishes
Egg Omelet with Prawns

This is a Chinese version of a Spanish omelet with plenty of prawns.

Ingredients:
200 g (7 oz.) black tiger prawns
  1/2 egg white
  2 teaspoons cornstarch
8 eggs
  2/3 teaspoon salt
  2 teaspoons sugar
Oil for deep-frying
3 tablespoons salad oil
Parsley for garnish

Method:
1. Remove shell, heads, and black veins from the back of prawns and cut into 1 cm-(1/2 inch-) thick pieces. (1–2)
2. Place prawn pieces in a bowl, add egg white and cornstarch, and mix well with hands. (3)
3. Fill a wok 70% full of oil and heat to medium high. Add prawn pieces. When they turn red, remove from pan. (2)
4. Beat eggs well with salt and sugar.
5. Clean the wok. Heat 3 tablespoons of salad oil in a wok. Pour egg mixture in, and stir-fry, scrambling. Stir in prawns quickly. (4)
6. Stir-fry eggs, flipping over once with spatula. (5)
7. Cut into 4 pieces. Arrange on serving plate, and garnish with parsley.

Fried Eggs in "Fu-ru"

Ingredients:

8 eggs
2 tablespoons red type, fermented bean
    curd cake 紅腐乳 (*hong-fu-ru*)   (A)
Seasonings:
    2 tablespoons chicken broth
    2 teaspoons sugar
    1/2 teaspoon sesame oil
    Dash of salt
3–4 tablespoons salad oil
2 tablespoons minced green onions or
    scallions

Method:

1. Beat the eggs in a bowl and add
hong-fu-ru first. Blend well and add
seasonings, including soup. Mix.   (1–2)
2. Heat 3 tablespoons salad oil in wok.
Pour in beaten egg mixture (1), and
cook, flipping over with large spatula.
Stop heat while the eggs are still soft.
    (3)
3. Arrange on plate and sprinkle with
minced green onions.

Notes:

"*Fu-ru*" 腐乳 is a tofu (bean curd) fermented in salt, seasonings and spices.
There are several kinds. The white type,
called white *fu-ru* or *bai-fu-ru* 白腐乳,
can be eaten as is with rice or rice
porridge. The red type, called *hong-
fu-ru* 紅腐乳, can not only be eaten as
is but also used as a seasoning. It has
a strong smell and tastes rather salty.
Available in bottles or cans.

58

Marbled Egg in Tea

This is a savory egg dish, prettily marbled with tea and soy sauce. This may take some trouble to make, but it adds color to the table.

Ingredients:

8 eggs
Seasonings:
   2 teaspoons tea leaves
   1 star anise
   1 tablespoon soy sauce
   1/2 teaspoon salt
   1 teaspoon sugar

Method:

1. Hard-boil the eggs. Tap egg shells lightly with back of spoon, so they have fine fissures. (1)

2. Put eggs in a pot. Add tea leaves, star anise and other seasonings. Pour water to cover. (2)

3. Place pot over medium heat. Cook until eggs turn brown, turning over with chopsticks occasionally. (3)

4. Remove shell carefully.

Meat Dishes

Steamed Chicken with Chili Sauce

This sauce, made with a mixture of garlic, ginger, and green onion, stimulates the appetite. A sharply flavored dish like this adds a refreshing accent to plain-tasting porridge.

Ingredients:
2 chicken thighs with bones
   1/2 stalk green onion
   1/2 piece of fresh ginger
1 tablespoon Chinese rice wine or saké
2 cucumbers
Sauce:
   3 tablespoons soy sauce
   2 tablespoons vinegar
   1/2 teaspoon chili pepper oil
   1/2 teaspoon sesame oil
   1/2 teaspoon pepper powder 花椒
     (hua-jiao)
   1 clove garlic, minced
   1 tablespoon minced green onions
   1 teaspoon minced fresh ginger

Method:
1. Arrange the chicken thighs in a skillet and pound the green onion and ginger with the back of a heavy knife a few times. (1)
2. Sprinkle rice wine over the chicken, place on plate, and put it into a prepared steamer. Steam over high heat for about 20 minutes. (2)
3. When the chicken is a little cool, tear it into pieces 6–7 milimeter or chopstick width. (3)
4. In a small bowl, mix the sauce ingredients. Add everything: garlic, green onions, and ginger. (4)
5. Slice cucumbers thin, and arrange on a plate. Place chicken over the cucumbers and pour the sauce over it. (4)

Deep-Fried Chicken in Sauce

Fried chicken is flavored twice with sauce. This is a hearty dish.

Ingredients:

800 g (1-3/4 lb.) chicken thighs with
  bones

Marinade:
  4 tablespoons soy sauce
  1 tablespoon sugar
  2 tablespoons Chinese rice wine
    or saké
  2 teaspoons ginger juice
3 tablespoons cornstarch
Oil for deep-frying
Seasoning mixture:
  3 tablespoons vinegar
  2 tablespoons sugar
  2 tablespoons soy sauce
  2 tablespoons chicken broth
4–5 lettuce leaves for garnish

Method:

1. Cut chicken thighs into bite-sized pieces with heavy knife. (1)

2. Mix marinade ingredients in a bowl, and add chicken pieces. Mix well, and marinate for about 20 minutes. (2)

3. When chicken pieces have absorbed the marinade well, wipe them with a paper towel. Coat with cornstarch and deep-fry in hot oil until crisp. Drain well on paper. (3)

4. Clean the wok, add the seasoning mixture and place it over heat. When it comes to a boil, add fried chicken and stir-fry quickly. (4)

5. Arrange the lettuce leaves on a serving plate, and place chicken on them.

Stewed Chicken Livers

It is important to get fresh livers, and to remove the blood from them well.

Ingredients:
8 chicken livers
2 slices fresh ginger
1 leek, 10 cm (4 inches) in length
1 star anise
Seasoning mixture:
  1 tablespoon sugar
  1 tablespoon Chinese rice wine
    or saké
  2 tablespoons soy sauce
  1 cup water

Method:
1. Divide each chicken liver in two, and remove coagulated blood and white strings. (1)
2. Put livers in a bowl and wash them well in running water, until the water runs clear. (2–3)
3. Place livers in an earthenware or other heavy pot. Add leek, which has been pounded with the back of a knife, ginger, star anise and seasoning mixture. (4)
4. Pour in 1 cup of water, cover with lid, and heat over high heat. When it comes to a boil, reduce heat and simmer for about 30 minutes until liquid is gone.
5. When cooked, cut livers into bite-sized pieces, and place them on a serving plate.

Stewed Gizzards

Gizzards, when cooked for a long time, taste crisp and pleasant on the tongue. This dish can be served not only as part of a meal, but also as a snack to accompany drinks.

Ingredients:
15 chicken gizzards
3 cm (1 inch) piece, fresh ginger
1 leek, 10 cm (4-inch) in length
1 star anise
Seasonings:
   1 tablespoon sugar
   1 tablespoon Chinese rice wine
     or saké
   3 tablespoons soy sauce

Method:
1. Boil plenty of water in a pot, and cook the gizzards quickly. Remove them from water. (1)
2. Remove gizzard fats in running water, and drain in a colander. (2)
3. Slice the ginger thinly, and pound ginger and leek with back of a knife.
4. Place the gizzards in an earthenware or other heavy pot. Add leek, ginger, star anise and seasonings, and add water a little less than needed to cover. (3)
5. Cover with lid, and put pot over high heat. When it comes to a boil, reduce heat and simmer until the liquid is gone.
6. When cooked and slightly cooled, slice gizzards lengthwise, and arrange on a serving plate. (4)

Stewed Beef

Beef shin meat is cooked slowly in a stock made with sugar, soy sauce and star anise. Beef is first boiled to remove blood and then cooked, which is the secret of the delicious taste.

Ingredients:
600 g (1-1/3 lb.) beef shin meat
1 leek, 10 cm (4-inch) in length
1 slice 2–3 mm-(1/10 inch-) thick ginger
1 star anise
Seasonings:
   2 tablespoons sugar
   4 tablespoons soy sauce
   2 tablespoons Chinese rice wine
     or saké
1 bunch spinach
1 cup water
1 teaspoon salt
2 tablespoons salad oil

Method:
1. Tie the beef with strings at several places.
2. Boil plenty of water in a pot, and put in the beef. Boil for just a while and remove. (To remove the blood.)
                        (1)
3. Pound leek and ginger with the back of a heavy knife. (2)
4. Put the beef in an earthenware or other heavy pot. Add leek and ginger, star anise and seasonings. Pour 2 cups of water over it. (3)
5. Cover and cook over medium-high heat until it comes to a boil. Then reduce heat, and simmer for about 2 hours until the meat becomes tender. Turn over occasionally, so the meat is seasoned evenly. (4)
6. When the beef is a little cool, slice thinly.
7. Wash the spinach thoroughly without cutting, and sauté in 2 tablespoons oil over high heat. Add salt and water, cover with a lid and cook until tender. Drain and place on a serving plate.
8. Arrange the beef on top.

Soybean Flavored Pork

The finished result has a sweet and sour taste. Pork goes well with green peppers.

Ingredients:
350 g (3/4 lb.) leg of pork (fresh ham)
  1/2 egg white
  1 tablespoon cornstarch
2 green peppers
1 red pepper
1 tablespoon minced green onions
1 teaspoon minced fresh ginger
1 teaspoon minced garlic
Seasoning mixture:
  1-1/2 tablespoons soy sauce
  2 tablespoons sugar
  1 tablespoon sweet brown bean paste (*tian-mian-jiang*) 甜麵醬
  1-1/2 tablespoons brown bean paste (*dou-ban-jiang*) 豆板醬
Oil for deep-frying
2 tablespoons salad oil

Method:
1. Slice the pork into strips. Coat them with beaten egg white and then with cornstarch, and mix well by hand.
2. Fill wok 70% with oil and heat to 90–100°C (210°F.). Deep-fry the pork until done. Drain oil.
3. Cut the green peppers in half lengthwise. Remove seeds, and slice thinly.
4. Heat 2 tablespoons salad oil in a wok over high heat, sauté green onions, ginger, and garlic. Add green peppers and stir-fry quickly. Add the deep-fried pork and seasoning mixture and stir-fry.

Deep-Fried Pork and Pickled Vegetables

Use pickled or preserved vegetables. If too salty, soak them in water.

Ingredients:
300 g (2/3 lb.) leg of pork (fresh ham)
  1/2 egg white
  2 teaspoons cornstarch
  Oil for deep-frying
200 g (7 oz.) pickled vegetables
2 tablespoons salad oil
Seasonings:
  1 tablespoon sugar
  1/4 teaspoon salt
  1 tablespoon Chinese rice wine
    or saké
  2–3 drops sesame oil

Method:
1. Cut pork into strips, and coat with egg white and cornstarch, and mix them well by hand. Half-fill a wok with oil. Deep-fry quickly at low temperature.
2. Wash pickled vegetables in water quickly, and drain. Cut into 5 cm- (2 inch-) long pieces.
3. Heat 2 tablespoons salad oil in a wok. Sauté pickled vegetables in wok, sprinkle with sugar and salt. Sauté again. Add pork and sprinkle with rice wine. Stir quickly and sprinkle with sesame oil to finish.

Stewed Ground Pork and Giant White Radish

Giant white radish stewed with dried shrimp and ground pork has a rich taste. Giant white radish becomes even more delicious cooked this way.

Ingredients:

2 tablespoons dried shrimp
600 g (1-1/3 lb.) giant white radish
1 teaspoon minced fresh ginger
1 tablespoon minced green onions
150 g (1/3 lb.) ground pork
Seasoning liquid:
   1 tablespoon Chinese rice wine
     or saké
   2 tablespoons soy sauce
   1 tablespoon sugar
   1 cup chicken broth
2 tablespoons salad oil

Method:

1. Wash the dried shrimp quickly and soak in water until soft. Mince finely.
2. Cut the giant white radish length-wise, and slice into bite-sized pieces.
(1)
3. Heat 2 tablespoons salad oil in a wok, and sauté ginger and green onions. When it begins to smell fragrant, add shrimp and sauté quickly.
4. Add ground pork and stir-fry. Add giant white radish and stir-fry again.
(2–3)
5. Add liquid ingredients. Cover with a lid and reduce heat to low. Cook for 30 minutes until giant white radish becomes tender. (4)

Seafood Dishes

Marinated Fish Fries

Fish is fried crisply, after being marinated well. This is good even cool, since the fish is seasoned rather strongly. In China, fresh-water fish such as carp are used, but mackerel, Spanish mackerel and skipjack are also good prepared this way.

Ingredients:
600 g (1-1/3 lb.) mackerel fillets
10 cm (4 inch) long green onion
2 slices fresh ginger
Seasonings:
   1/2 cup Chinese rice wine or saké
   1/2 cup soy sauce
   1/3 cup sugar
Oil for deep-frying
Lettuce leaves for garnish

Method:
1. Pound green onion and ginger with back of knife, and place them in a deep bowl or skillet. Add seasonings and mix well.
2. Marinate mackerel pieces in marinade. Turn them over occasionally, so they absorb it evenly. Let stand for about 4 hours. (1)
3. Fill wok 70% with oil and heat to medium temperature. Dry mackerel pieces with paper towel. (2–3)
4. Deep-fry mackerel pieces over medium heat, until they are done. Raise heat to high at the end to make them crisp.
5. Drain oil well, and serve on lettuce leaves spread on a plate.

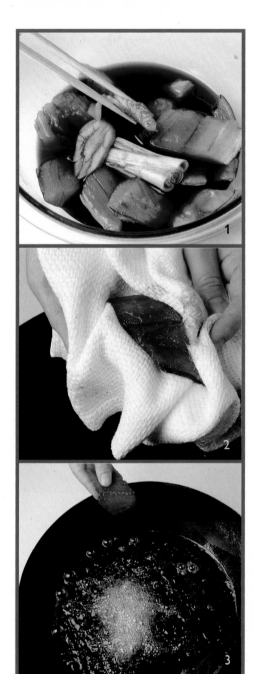

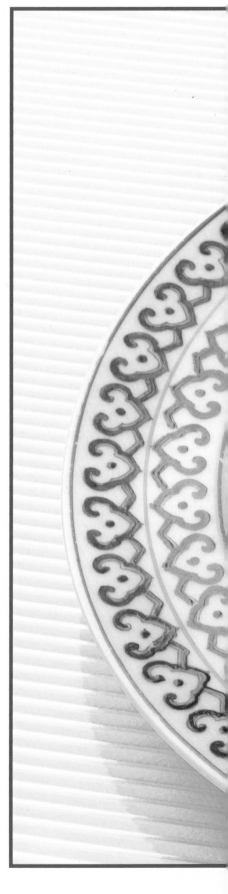

Deep-Fried Fish in Ketchup

This is a Cantonese dish, with tabasco mixed in ketchup making it spicy. This dish has an onion flavor.

Ingredients:
450 g (1 lb.) white-meat fish
Marinade:
   1 tablespoon Chinese rice wine
     or saké
   1 tablespoon soy sauce
   2–3 drops sesame oil
   Dash of pepper
1/2 egg, beaten
Cornstarch for dusting
1 onion
Seasonings:
   1/2 cup chicken broth
   2 tablespoons tomato ketchup
   1 teaspoon tabasco
   1-1/2 teaspoons sugar
   1 teaspoon salt
   2–3 drops sesame oil
   Dash of pepper
2 teaspoons cornstarch dissolved
   in 4 teaspoons water
2 tablespoons salad oil
Oil for deep-frying

Method:
1. Remove bones from white-meat fish with tweezers. Remove skin, and cut into rather big rectangular pieces. (1–2)
2. Place fish in a skillet. Add marinade and let stand for about 10 minutes. (3)
3. Cut onion in half lengthwise, and slice into 7 mm-(1/3 inch-) thick pieces.
4. In a bowl mix the seasonings well.
5. Beat egg. Dip the fish pieces in beaten egg and dust with cornstarch lightly. Fill deep pan 70% full with oil and deep-fry fish at high temperature until golden brown.
6. Heat salad oil in a wok, and sauté onions lightly. Add fish and seasonings. Mix well to season the fish thoroughly. (4)
7. Thicken with dissolved cornstarch.

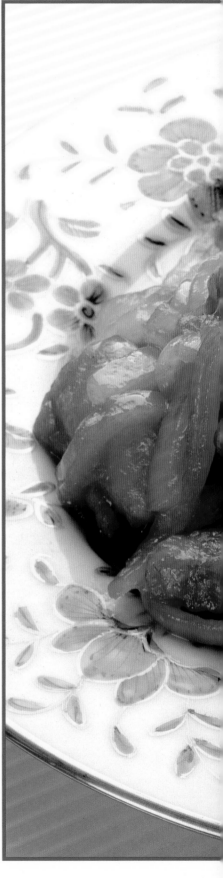

Stir-Fried Prawns and Green Peas

This dish has a pleasing appearance combining the green of green peas and the pink of prawns. It is a light-tasting dish. Prawns are coated with egg whites, deep-fried and then pan-fried, so they become fluffy.

Ingredients:
160 g (1/3 lb.) prawns
   1/2 egg white
   2 teaspoons cornstarch
300 g (2/3 lb.) frozen green peas
1 piece of fresh ginger, thinly sliced
Seasonings:
   1 teaspoon salt
   1/2 teaspoon sugar
   1 tablespoon Chinese rice wine
     or saké
   Dash of pepper
2 tablespoons salad oil
Oil for deep-frying

Method:
1. Shell prawns and remove black veins in the back. Wash well and drain.
(1–2)
2. Place prawns in a bowl. Add egg white and cornstarch and mix well by hand.
3. Half-fill wok with oil and deep fry prawns over medium heat. Stir them with chopsticks to separate them. When prawns turn red, remove them with strainer and drain off oil. (3–5)
4. Thaw green peas in hot water.
5. Heat 2 tablespoons salad oil in a wok. Sauté ginger. Add green peas and stir-fry quickly. Then add prawns and stir-fry quickly. (6–7)
6. Add seasonings, and mix well.

Sichuan-Style Prawn Fries

This is a dish of prawn fries, born in Szechuan and perfected in Canton. Prawns curl up like flowers if they are opened in the back and fried. Either tabasco or brown bean paste 豆板醬 (*dou-ban-jiaing*) can be used.

Ingredients:
12 prawns
1 teaspoon minced garlic
Seasoning mixture:
   1/2 cup chicken broth
   1/2 cup tomato ketchup
   2 tablespoons sugar
   1 teaspoon salt
   1 teaspoon tabasco or brown
     bean paste (*dou-ban-jiaing*)
2 tablespoons salad oil
2 teaspoons cornstarch dissolved in
   4 teaspoons water
Oil for deep-frying

Method:
1. Shell prawns, leaving the tails. Slit lengthwise down the back of prawns and devein. (1–3)
2. Cut off the tips of the tails, push out water from tails using dull edge of knife so they will fry without crackling. (4)
3. Fill wok 70% full with oil and heat to medium-high. Dry prawns well with paper towel and put them in oil. When they turn red, remove them from the wok immediately. (5)
4. In a bowl combine seasoning mixture well.
5. Clean the wok. Heat 2 tablespoons fresh salad oil and sauté garlic. Pour in seasoning mixture. Bring to a boil. Add prawns and stir-fry. (7)
6. Thicken with dissolved cornstarch.

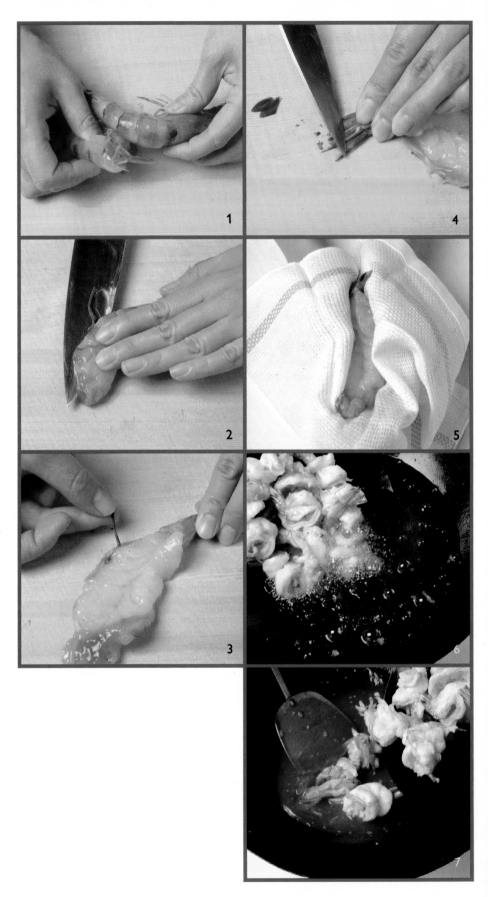

Vinegared Squid and Celery

Squid is scored to improve appearance and for easier digestion. Boil squid quickly and place in cold water. If overcooked, squid becomes tough.

Ingredients:
1 squid
3 stalks celery
Vinegar mixture:
   3 tablespoons vinegar
   2 tablespoons sugar
   1 tablespoon soy sauce
   1 teaspoon brown bean paste
     (*dou-ban-jiang*)
   1/2 teaspoon salt
   2–3 drops sesame oil

Method:
1. Remove tentacles from squid by pulling slowly so that ink does not squirt out. Remove internal organs. (1)

2. Cut squid open lengthwise into one flat piece. (2)

3. Remove skin carefully. If difficult, rub off it with tightly squeezed wet towel. (3)

4. Cut into half lengthwise. Score, first, lengthwise, making lines 5 mm (1/5 inch) apart. Then, sideways, making lines 5 mm (1/5 inch) apart. Cut into bite-sized pieces. (The scoring should be slanted and 2/3 of the way through the squid meat.) (4–5)

5. Boil water in a pot, and add squid pieces. Boil lightly, and when the scord section open, put squid into cold water, and drain in colander. (6)

6. Remove strings from celery stalks. Cut stalks into thin pieces 5 cm (2 inch) in length.

7. Put vinegar mixture in a bowl, add squid and celery pieces and combine. Marinate well about 1 hour.

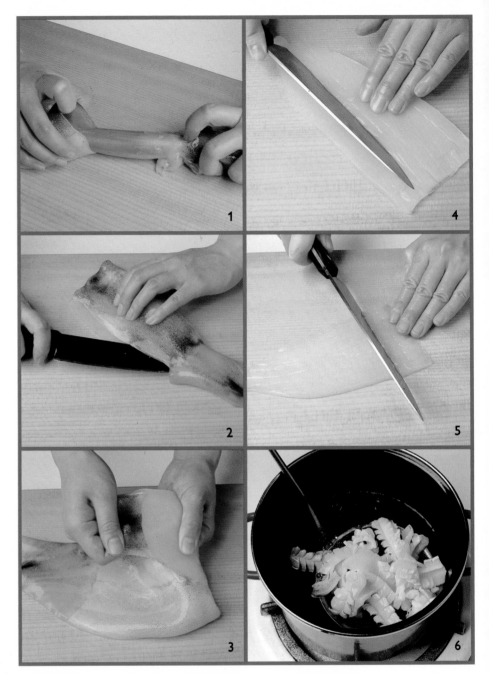

Oyster Stew with Ginger

This is a perfect dish to accompany porridge—it is seasoned strongly, and flavored with ginger. This useful dish will keep a long time.

Ingredients:
500 g (1-1/4 lb.) shelled oysters
100 g (3-1/2 oz.) fresh ginger
Seasonings:
  1/4 cup Chinese rice wine or saké
  2 tablespoons soy sauce
  2 tablespoons sugar
  1 teaspoon oyster sauce
2 tablespoons salad oil

Method:
1. Remove broken shell pieces and wash oysters well by swishing them in water. Drain.
2. Cut ginger into long, thin strips.
3. Heat 2 tablespoons salad oil in a wok, and sauté ginger. Add oysters and stir-fry lightly and remove them to a plate.
4. Put wok over heat again. Add seasonings and bring to a boil. Add oysters and ginger and cover with a lid, and simmer until the liquid is gone.

Steamed Clams with "Dou-chi"

This dish has the savory flavor of fermented soy beans 豆豉 (*dou-chi*). Clams are served in shells, so this is a perfect dish for a special menu for guests.

Ingredients:
12 clams
1 tablespoon minced green onion
2 teaspoons minced fresh ginger
1 tablespoon fermented soy beans

豆豉 (*dou-chi*)
1 tablespoon Chinese rice wine or saké
1 teaspoon sugar
1 teaspoon soy sauce
2 tablespoons salad oil
Chinese parsley for garnish

Method:
1. Wash clams in water, and soak them in lightly salted water overnight so they discharge any sand. Open shells and remove clam.
2. Mince fermented soy beans.
3. Heat 2 tablespoons salad oil in a wok, and sauté green onions, ginger, and fermented soy beans, When mixture starts to smell fragrant, place each clam on a shell-side.
4. Sprinkle rice wine, sugar, and soy sauce over clams to season. Cover, and steam for awhile until clams are done. Arrange on serving plate and garnish with Chinese parsley.

Bean Curd Dishes
Bean Curd and Greens

This is a colorful and elegant bean curd soup, white, red, and green, which combines many ingredients. Serve in a deep dish.

Ingredients:
2 blocks soft bean curd (*dou-fu*)
  (*tofu* in Japanese)
150 g (1/3 lb.) shrimp
  1/2 egg white
  1 teaspoon cornstarch
100 g (3-1/2 lb.) edible chrysanthemum
  greens
Seasonings:
  1/2 cup chicken broth
  2/3 teaspoon salt
  1/2 teaspoon sugar
  1 tablespoon Chinese rice wine
    or saké
2 teaspoons cornstarch dissolved
  in 4 teaspoons water
2 tablespoons salad oil
Oil for deep-frying

Method:
1. Cut bean curd into 1 cm (1/2 inch) cubes. Place them in a slanted skillet, to let water drain off naturally. (1)
2. Shell shrimp. Remove heads and black veins. Wash and drain. Coat with egg whites and then cornstarch. Fill wok 70% full with oil and heat to medium. Deep-fry shrimp quickly. (2)
3. Boil chrysanthemum greens in hot water and cool in cold water. Squeeze to remove water, and cut them into bite-sized pieces. (2)
4. Heat 2 tablespoons salad oil in wok over high heat, and sauté bean curd. Add shrimps and chrysanthemum leaves and stir-fry quickly. (3)
5. Add seasoning mixture, cover with lid, and cook over low heat for 15 minutes. Thicken with dissolved cornstarch. (4)

Bean Curd Stew

Ingredients:

2 blocks soft bean curd
150 g (1/3 lb.) pork, sliced
1 small bamboo shoot, boiled
5–6 dried Chinese mushrooms
1 red chili pepper
1 teaspoon minced garlic

Seasoning mixture:
   2/3 cup soup stock
   1/4 teaspoon salt
   1-1/2 teaspoons sugar
2 tablespoons sweet brown bean paste
   甜麵醬 (*tian-mian-jiang*)
2 tablespoons soy sauce
1 tablespoon Chinese rice wine
2–3 drops sesame oil
2 teaspoons cornstarch dissolved
   in 4 teaspoons water
2 tablespoons salad oil
Oil for deep-frying

Method:

1. Cut bean curd into 1 cm (1/2 inch) cubes, and let water drain naturally in a slanted pan.

2. Cut pork and bamboo shoots into bite-sized pieces. Soak dried mushrooms in water for 30 minutes until they absorb water, then squeeze out excess. Remove the hard stems, and cut mushrooms in half.

3. Remove seeds from red pepper chili and cut into small pieces.

4. Half-fill wok with oil and heat to medium. Deep-fry bean curd and pork. Drain.

5. Clean the wok. Heat 2 tablespoons salad oil, and sauté garlic. Add, in this order, bamboo shoot, mushrooms, red chili pepper, bean curd, and pork, and stir-fry.

6. Add seasoning mixture, and stir-fry. Thicken with dissolved constarch.

Bean Curd and Mustard Greens Salad

Adjust the amount of salt used, depending on the saltiness of the pickles. When pickles are too salty, soak them in water for awhile before frying.

Ingredients:
1 block regular bean curd
100 g (3-1/2 oz.) pickled mustard leaves
2 tablespoons salad oil

Seasonings:
  1/2 teaspoon salt
  1 teaspoon soy sauce
  1 teaspoon sugar

Method:
1. Cut bean curd into 1 cm (1/2 inch) cubes. Boil them quickly in hot water. Drain in a colander and let them cool.
2. Wash pickles and squeeze out water. Mince.
3. In a wok, heat 2 tablespoons salad oil and sauté pickles lightly. Add seasoning mixture and stir-fry lightly. Place them on plate and let cool.
4. In a bowl combine bean curd and sautéed pickles carefully so bean curd doesn't break.
5. Arrange on a plate.

Processed Food Dishes

Marinated Red Kidney Beans

Choose a can of red kidney beans which is not sweetened. This marinated dish is good for one's health.

Ingredients:
1 can (about 450 g; 1 lb.) red kidney beans (unsweetened)
1/2 cup chopped celery
1 tablespoon minced Szechuan preserved vegetables 搾菜 (*zha-cai*)
Seasonings:
    4 tablespoons vinegar
    4 tablespoons sugar
    1 tablespoon soy sauce
    1 tablespoon mustard
    1 tablespoon sesame oil

Method:
1. Drain can of red kidney beans. (1)
2. Soak preserved vegetables in water to remove saltiness and bitterness and dice them in rather large pieces. (2–3)
3. Mix seasonings in a bowl well. Add red kidney beans, preserved vegetables, and ingredients. Combine and marinate for 1 hour, stirring occasionally so the flavor is absorbed.

Stir-Fried "Zha-cai" and Dried Shrimp

This is a side dish which combines well the savory shrimp and the spiciness of preserved vegetables (*zha-cai*).

Ingredients:
1 piece preserved vegetable
  (*zha-cai*)
3 tablespoons dried shrimp

Seasoning mixture:
  1/2 teaspoon salt
  1 teaspoon sugar
  2–3 drops sesame oil
1 tablespoon salad oil

Method:
1. Soak preserved vegetable in water for a while, to remove its saltiness and spiciness Cut into thin pieces.
2. Wash dried shrimp quickly, soak in water until soft and remove. Chop.
3. Heat 2 tablespoons salad oil in a wok. Add preserved vegetable and dried shrimp, and stir-fry. Add seasoning mixture.

Note: Adjust the amount of salt, depending on the saltiness of the preserved vegetable.

Cooked Chinese Mushrooms

Thick Chinese mushrooms are cooked a long time. Oyster sauce adds a special flavor to the dish.

Ingredients:
20 small dried Chinese mushrooms
2 tablespoons salad oil
Sauce:
   3 tablespoons chicken broth
   1 tablespoon oyster sauce
   1 teaspoon soy sauce
   2 teaspoons sugar
   2–3 drops sesame oil
   Dash of pepper

Method:
1. Soak dried mushrooms in water until soft. Remove the hard stems.
2. Heat 2 tablespoons salad oil in a wok. Sauté mushrooms, add all other ingredients and cover. Simmer over low heat until there is no liquid.

DESSERTS AND SNACKS

Chinese Desserts & Snacks

Rice Flour Dumplings with Fruit in Syrup

This is a punch-style dessert, with colorful fruit and white dumplings. Cool well, and serve in a glass bowl for a party menu. Liquor can be added for a different taste.

Ingredients:
Dumplings:
   100 g (3 1/2 oz.) rice flour
   1 cup water
10 strawberries
1/2 papaya
1 kiwi fruit
1 lime
Syrup:
   1 cup sugar
   3 cups water

Method:
1. Dissolve sugar in water in a small pan over low heat. Cool in refrigerator.
2. Put the rice flour in a bowl, add water little by little and mix well. When mixture becomes soft, form into small dumplings. (1–2)
3. Boil plenty of water in a pot, and drop in dumplings. Boil a little more after dumplings come up to surface. Scoop them out and put them into cool water. (3–4)
4. Wash and remove crowns of strawberries. (Cut big berries in half.) Peel papaya and remove seeds, and cut into pieces of equal size. Peel kiwi. Cut in half, and then slice. Slice lime thinly.
5. Put dumplings and the fruits in a glass bowl. Add syrup.

Tapioca and Yam Soup

Enjoy the feel of tapioca grains on the tongue as well as the flavor of coconut milk. This is a delicious sweet dish, hot or cold.

Ingredients:
250 g (9 oz.) taro yam
1/2 cup tapioca
1 cup coconut milk
3 cups milk
2 cups sugar

Method:
1. Steam taro yam whole with skin, until soft. Peel while warm, and mash it. (1)
2. Soak tapioca for about 30 minutes to absorb water. Boil until soft. Drain.
3. Pour coconut milk, regular milk, and sugar into taro mixture and mix well. Add tapioca. Cool and serve. (2)

Sweet Sesame Soup

This is a Chinese sweet soup, with the flavor of sesame seeds. Black sesame seeds are often used in China because they make hair glossy and skin bright, and also because they are good for one's health. This is a delicious sweet soup, hot or cold.

Ingredients:
70 g (2-1/2 oz.) black sesame seeds
1 cup rock sugar
2 cups water
1 tablespoon cornstarch dissolved in 2 tablespoons water

Method:
1. Toast sesame seeds in a small pan, and grind them in a mortar or food processor. (3–4)
2. Put rock sugar and water in a pot and place over heat. When rock sugar dissolves, add ground sesame seeds.
3. Strain soup and make it smooth. Put over heat again. When it becomes warm, add dissolved cornstarch, stir to thicken. (5–6)

Steamed Rice Dumplings

Rice flour dumplings with red bean jam are covered with glutinous rice and fried. Use drained rice, otherwise it won't adhere to the dumplings.

Ingredients:
200 g (7 oz.) rice flour
   About 1 cup water
For red bean jam:
   1-1/2 cups sugar
   1 cup water
   1/2 cup powdered or red bean paste
   2 tablespoons lard
   1/8 teaspoon salt
A little more than 1 cup of
   glutinous rice
Candied cherries for garnish

Method:
1. Soak glutinous rice in water over-night and drain well in a colander.
2. Put sugar and water in a pot. Add red powdered bean paste when sugar dissolves. Stir with wooden spatula. Add lard and salt, and stir again to bring out luster. (1)
3. Little by little add water by hand to rice flour in a bowl. Knead until it gets smooth and soft. Roll it into a bar and cut into 12 pieces. (2)
4. Divide red bean paste into 12 por-tions, and make each portion into a ball.
5. Shape the 12 dough pieces into balls. Flatten them, and wrap up each red bean pasteball in dough. (3)
6. Roll dumplings in glutinous rice. Cover them evenly, and top with a piece of cherry. (4)
7. Place dumplings in steamer and steam for about 15 minutes over high heat. (5)

Banana Fritters

The fluffy egg white coating and sweet bananas make a splendid combination. If left for a long time after they are fried, the coating shrivels, so serve them hot right from the frying pan.

Ingredients:
4 bananas
Batter:
   3 egg whites
   3/4 cup flour
Jam of your favorite fruit—
   apricot, apple, blueberry, etc.
Powdered sugar
Oil for frying

Method:
1. In a bowl, beat egg whites until stiff. (1)
2. Sift flour into egg whites, and mix lightly. (2)
3. Peel bananas and cut them into slanted 5 mm-(1/5 inch-) thick pieces. Sandwich jam between two pieces. (3)
4. Coat banana sandwiches with batter. Fill a wok 70% full of oil, heat to medium high and deep-fry until fluffy. Drain. Arrange on plate and sprinkle with powdered sugar. (4)

Roast Pork Pie

Chinese pies are made in a way similar to Western pies. Lard is used instead of butter. Frozen pastry sheets are used in this recipe to make it easier.

Ingredients:
4 frozen pastry sheets, 20 × 20 cm
   (8 × 8 inch)
100 g (3-1/2 oz.) roast pork
2 tablespoons minced green onions
Seasoning mixture:
   1 tablespoon soy sauce
   3 tablespoons sugar
   1 tablespoon Hoisin sauce or
      brown-red sweet bean-paste
      sauce (*hai-hsien-chiang*)
   1/2 tablespoon oyster sauce
   1/2 cup chicken broth
   2–3 drops sesame oil
   Dash of pepper
1 tablespoon salad oil
2 teaspoons cornstarch dissolved
   in 4 teaspoons water
1 egg yolk
Some white sesame seeds

Method:
1. Dice roast pork into 1 cm (1/2 inch) cubes.
2. Heat 1 tablespoon salad oil in a wok, and sauté green onions. When they become fragrant, add roast pork and stir-fry. Add seasoning mixture.
(1)
3. Stir-fry quickly, add dissolved cornstarch to thicken. Transfer to plate and cool. (2)
4. Cut pie sheets (thaw if frozen) into 4 pieces, and spoon cooled filling onto each sheet. Fold in two, to form rectangular or triangular pieces, and press edges together. Make patterns on edges with fork. (3–4)
5. Place pastries on a greased baking sheet, leaving space in between so sides of pastries barely touch. Spread egg yolk on surface with brush, sprinkle with white sesame seeds. (5)
6. Preheat oven to 200°C. (390°F.) and bake for 15 minutes until light brown.

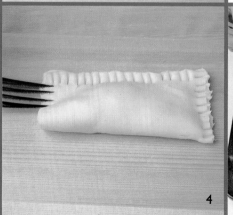

Spring Rolls

Ingredients: (4–5 servings)
10 spring roll sheets
Spring roll fillings:
   200 g (7 oz.) ground pork
   30 g (1 oz.) dried bean thread
     noodles
   100 g straw mushrooms, canned
   2 tablespoons minced green onions
   1 teaspoon minced fresh ginger
Seasoning mixture:
   1 tablespoon Chinese rice wine
   2 tablespoons soy sauce
   1 tablespoon sugar
   2 teaspoons oyster sauce
2 teaspoons cornstarch, dissolved
   in 4 teaspoons water
Sweet and sour sauce:
   1/2 cup vinegar/1/2 cup sugar
   1 teaspoon salt
   1 teaspoon tabasco
   1 red chili pepper, seeds
     removed and minced
1 head lettuce for garnish
Oil for deep-frying flour

Method:

1. Soak bean thread noodles in hot water to soften, and cut them finely. (1)

2. Mince straw mushrooms.

3. Heat 2 tablespoons salad oil in a wok, and sauté green onions and ginger. When soft, add ground pork, and stir-fry over low heat. Add bean threads noodles and straw mushrooms. Stir-fry quickly, add seasoning mixture and mix. (2)

4. Thicken with dissolved cornstarch. Transfer to plate and cool.

5. Spread spring roll sheets flat and spoon cooled filling in center. Place flour dissolved in water along edges so they will stick together. Fold edges in two, then roll them up. (3–4)

6. Fill wok 70% full with oil and heat to high temperature. Deep-fry spring rolls (5) until crisp.

7. Mix sweet and sour sauce ingredients in a bowl.

8. Arrange lettuce leaves on plate, and place spring rolls on top. Serve hot, with sweet and sour sauce.

KITCHEN UTENSILS

Wok

There are two kinds: with one handle or with two handles. Woks are suitable for stir- or deep-frying because the rounded bottom will heat evenly. For family use, it is best to choose a lightweight wok made of steel, with a diameter of 33–36 cm (13–14 in.).

It should be cleaned with hot water. If it is too dirty, liquid detergent can be used. After washing, it should be dried with a towel and then completely dried over a hot stove. (1, 2)

Steamer

This is made of bamboo. It releases steam nicely so it does not accumulate inside and food is beautifully steamed. It should be a little smaller than your wok so that it can sit firmly on the wok. It is possible to stack several steamers in layers. (3)

Ladle with holes

Chopped meat or fish are often fried very quickly in Chinese cooking. This ladle is useful to for removing them quickly from deep oil. A net ladle can be substituted. (4)

Chopping board

It is useful to have a larger chopping board in addition to your ordinary one. (5)

Cooking knife

A Chinese cooking knife is useful for chopping ginger or garlic and is big enough to hold ingredients on its surface. An ordinary cooking knife can be substituted at home, but it is desirable to have a Chinese cooking knife thick enough to cut rib meat. (6, 7)

Iron spatula and ladle

Metal spatula for stirring or turning over ingredients. A metal ladle can be used the same way and for ladling soup or oil as well. Ladles with longer handles are better. (8, 9)

Earthenware pot and glazed earthenware pan

An earthenware pot is used for boiling rice porridge, meat or vegetables. This conveys heat from the bottom evenly

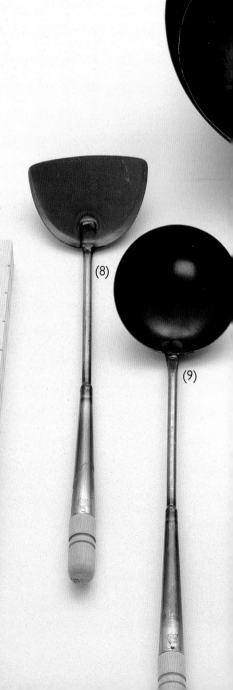

(5)

(6)

(7)

(8)

(9)

and retains warmth superbly.

A glazed earthenware pan is especially useful for rice porridge. Since it has a small mouth from which steam can escape, it will heat evenly and boil rice beautifully without boiling it over.

Make sure that the bottom is completely dry before heating. A sudden change of temperature may cause cracks. Therefore do not place hot earthenware vessels on a wet towel or in water. Do not place them suddenly on a strong flame. First heat them gradually, then put ingredients in and turn up the flame. (10, 11)

Index of Recipes